SUPER STRUCTURES OF THE WORLD

THINKING BIG:
AMERICA'S GREATEST CONSTRUCTIONS

BLACKBIRCH®
PRESS

San Diego • Detroit • New York • San Francisco • Cleveland • New Haven, Conn. • Waterville, Maine • London • Munich

THOMSON
GALE

LIBRARY OF CONGRESS CATALOGING–IN–PUBLICATION DATA

Thinking big / Elaine Pascoe, book editor.
    p. cm. — (Super structures of the world)
Summary: Explores the history and building of several major landmarks in America, including the Brooklyn Bridge, River Rouge industrial plant, the Empire State Building, and the Interstate Highway System.
Includes bibliographical references and index.
  ISBN 1-56711-870-4 — ISBN 1-4103-0193-1
  1. Structural engineering—United States—Juvenile literature. 2. Buildings—United States—Juvenile literature. [1. Structural engineering. 2. Building.] I. Pascoe, Elaine. II. Series.

TA634.T47 2004
624.1'0973—dc21
                                                 2003007521

Printed in China
10 9 8 7 6 5 4 3 2 1

THINKING BIG

America is home to some of the greatest buildings ever constructed. Not just mighty monuments and stunning skyscrapers, but buildings that are exciting, extraordinary, and sometimes even outrageous....

Get to know the brilliant architects, the inventive engineers, and the brave workers who together built the buildings that say AMERICA.

Above: The Statue of Liberty is an American monument and the country's first super structure.

Left: I-70, part of America's Interstate Highway System, goes through the Rocky Mountains from Colorado to California.

Right: Brilliant architects, engineers, and workers contributed their imagination, talent, and skill to create the Hoover Dam.

Left: Majestic skyscrapers now make up the skyline of America's greatest cities, but they were once only the ideas of architects and engineers.

Imagine New York City 150 years ago. It was the gateway to America. But it looked ragged and undistinguished, with low-rise housing and shops jostling for space and only an occasional church spire rising above the skyline.

Three thousand miles away in Paris, French artist Frederic Bertholdi had an idea that would give New York the symbol it needed. In 1875 he began work on a statue to celebrate one hundred years of American independence, a gift from the French people. It would have an ingenious skeleton of steel, clothed with panels of copper. No one had ever built such a creation before. It was an improbable dream, but only the first of many that would change New York over the next hundred years.

It wasn't until 1886 that enough money was raised for the statue to be completed. By that time Manhattan already had a famous landmark. . . .

Left: Only one hundred and fifty years ago, the Manhattan skyline was low and undistinguished, a far cry from the unique sight that greets visitors when they approach the island today.

THE BROOKLYN BRIDGE

A third of a mile from shore to shore, the Brooklyn Bridge has become one of the triumphant features of the New York skyline. Six lanes of roadway carry more than one hundred thousand cars a day high above the East River. Built in 1883, for half a century the Brooklyn Bridge was the longest in the world. Every suspension bridge built since that time owes its existence to this, the wonder of its day.

Before the bridge was built, Brooklyn and Manhattan were two different cities, separated by the East River. The only way to get from one to the other was by ferryboat. Would there ever be another way to cross the river?

Above: In 1883, the Brooklyn Bridge was the longest suspension bridge in the world and it held its title for fifty years after its completion.

Right: While French artist Frederic Bertholdi intended for the Statue of Liberty to be New York's first landmark, the Brooklyn Bridge was completed first.

Top: John Roebling designed the Brooklyn Bridge, which would traverse the East River from Manhattan to Brooklyn, as the longest suspension bridge in the world.

John Roebling, who manufactured wire cable, thought he knew another way: a suspension bridge—the world's longest suspension bridge. Roebling designed it, but no one knew if he could actually build it. If it came off it would be twice as long as any suspension bridge previously built.

It was John Roebling's son, Washington, who would take on the enormous task of making his father's dream come true. It would take him fourteen years.

Above: Heavy wire cables, manufactured by Roebling, held the weight of the Brooklyn Bridge.

The first problem was how to build the towers that support the bridge in seventy-five feet of water. The answer was a giant airtight wooden box called a caisson—essentially a giant inverted cup that trapped air. Workers in the caisson would dig down into the riverbed, to give the tower a solid footing, and the tower would be built on top of it.

Roebling's plan was to sink the caissons down to bedrock. It was ingenious—except for one thing. Mysteriously, over a hundred of Roebling's caisson workers became violently ill. Then they began to die.

The trapped air was becoming more and more compressed as the caisson went down. Roebling hadn't realized that compressed air was dangerous—no one had. There was no such thing as a decompression

chamber for workers returning to the surface, so they got what is now known as the bends. As they came up, nitrogen bubbles formed in their blood. Washington Roebling himself was paralyzed from the waist down by the bends. It didn't stop him. He carried on supervising construction from his house, with binoculars.

Above left: Workers in a caisson, an airtight wooden box, dug deep into the riverbed to create a solid foundation for the bridge.

Left: Washington Roebling continued his father's work on the Brooklyn Bridge, but a mysterious illness plagued his workers.

But Roebling realized he had to do something to stop the deaths, so he took a calculated risk. He stopped work with the tower actually resting on firm soil, above bedrock. Obviously it was a good decision—the bridge is still here.

When these giant towers, each 257 feet high, were completed, they were New York's first skyscrapers. But then Roebling came to the crunch. How was he going to get the cat's cradle of cables that would support the roadbed across the river? The wire cables would be too heavy to lift.

Top right: Because the wire cables were so heavy, Roebling had to determine how to suspend the cables across the river.

Middle: The towers of the Brooklyn Bridge were 257 feet high upon completion and became New York's first skyscrapers.

Bottom: The towers of the bridge rest on firm soil above bedrock in the East River.

Right: Roebling invented a shuttle wheel that carried the cable across the East River.

Left: Roebling's shuttle wheel has been vital to every suspension bridge built after the Brooklyn Bridge.

In a moment of pure genius, Roebling decided he could spin the cables in the sky. He invented a shuttle wheel that would run back and forth across the river carrying the cable, one wire at a time. Each wire was then looped round the anchors on either shore. It is this marvelous invention that made all future suspension bridges possible.

The suspension cables were Roebling's masterpiece. An intricate web of 380 wires hangs down to carry the weight of the roadway. So strong are the cables, the bridge could easily cope with many times the number of cars that surge across it each day.

Opposite page: With a complex web of 380 wires to hold it high above the river, the Brooklyn Bridge can handle much more than just the cars and trucks that cross it every day.

THE RIVER ROUGE PLANT

By the early twentieth century, automobile was changing America. And it was Henry Ford who made the automobile cheap and affordable. His Model T Ford was so successful that he had to come up with a completely new way of building cars to keep up with the enormous demand. Ford decided he would build a revolutionary factory that could do the whole job of building a car under one roof. Raw materials would go in one end; finished cars would come out the other. In 1917 he bought two thousand acres of swampland along the Rouge River on the outskirts of Detroit. His partners thought he was mad. Undaunted, Henry Ford built the largest industrial plant the world had ever seen.

Above left: Henry Ford made the first affordable automobile, the Model T.
Above right: Ford's Model T was so successful that he built a factory along the Rouge River, on the outskirts of Detroit, to produce enough cars to meet demand.

At Ford's own private docks freighters unloaded iron ore and coal, which went into the biggest foundry on earth to make steel. Giant steam hammers pounded the raw materials in to parts and engines. At the heart of Henry Ford's revolution was assembly plant B. Here Ford's revolutionary assembly line snaked back and forth over the unprecedented length of two and a half miles.

Henry Ford was now able to produce cars faster and cheaper than any of his rivals. The cost of the Ford cars fell to $375. Customers lapped them up. The age of the automobile had begun. Nearly half the cars on the planet were identical Ford Model T's. Henry Ford had truly put the world on wheels.

Above: Freighters brought iron ore and coal to Ford's private docks. At Ford's foundry, workers made these materials into steel.

Right: The two-and-a-half-mile-long assembly line enabled Ford to produce cars that cost only $375.

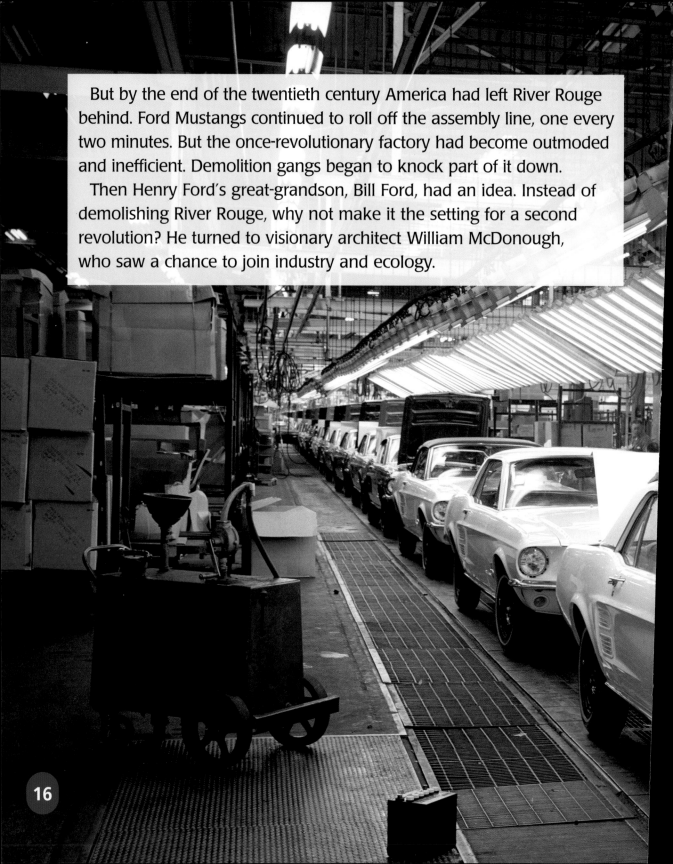

But by the end of the twentieth century America had left River Rouge behind. Ford Mustangs continued to roll off the assembly line, one every two minutes. But the once-revolutionary factory had become outmoded and inefficient. Demolition gangs began to knock part of it down.

Then Henry Ford's great-grandson, Bill Ford, had an idea. Instead of demolishing River Rouge, why not make it the setting for a second revolution? He turned to visionary architect William McDonough, who saw a chance to join industry and ecology.

Left: When the Rouge River factory became outdated, Bill Ford, Henry's grandson, enlisted architect William McDonough to revitalize it.

Far left: At the end of the twentieth century, the Rouge River factory produced one Ford Mustang every two minutes.

McDonough designed a new assembly building with the world's largest living roof—covered with soil and planted with sedum. The living plants will absorb carbon dioxide, reduce heat loss in winter, and cool naturally in summer. Huge skylights illuminate the assembly line below and reduce the need for electricity. Storm water from the site is channeled through a constructed wetland, where native plants purify it before it returns to the river. Ford will save somewhere between $8 million and $35 million over conventional storm-water treatment, so this is actually much less expensive than traditional methods.

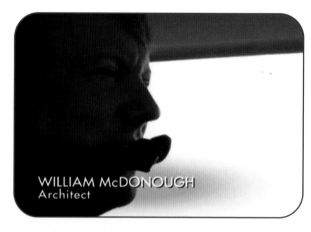

WILLIAM McDONOUGH
Architect

Top: McDonough designed the new Ford building as an ecological landmark in its own right. Above: The new building has the world's largest living roof, complete with soil and native plants.

Above: Huge columns support the building and keep it anchored to the ground.

Middle: McDonough views the building as a massive tree with the support columns acting as trunks.

Bottom: Large skylights allow sunlight to illuminate the assembly line below the roof.

The huge building is supported by sixteen hundred columns, driven seventy-five to one hundred feet in to the ground. McDonough compares the columns to tree trunks, supporting the leaves of the living roof. "Not only is the building like a tree, but it's a celebration of a whole new agenda that honors the abundance of the natural world," he says.

THE EMPIRE STATE BUILDING

New York, more than any other city, is defined by skyscrapers. And the building that symbolizes the New York skyline, and the very idea of skyscrapers all over the world, is the Empire State Building. The Empire State Building is more than seventy years old, and it's been a long time since it was the world's tallest building. But it's still the most famous skyscraper in the world.

Top right: New York City is a city of skyscrapers that tower high above pedestrians.

Right: The Empire State Building is a true New York landmark and one of the most famous skyscrapers in the world.

This page: The Empire State Building once stood taller than any other skyscraper in New York City and even claimed the title of the tallest building in the world.

The idea for the building was born in the boom years of the 1920s. Pressure for office space in Manhattan was leading to taller and taller buildings. Building the biggest brought prestige and profits. For a time it seemed that the prize would go to carmaker Walter Chrysler for his magnificent Lexington Avenue structure, at 1,048 feet the tallest building in the world. But even as the Chrysler Building opened its doors in 1929, architects were at work on an even taller skyscraper.

Above: As Manhattan became more crowded and the need for office space grew, architects began to build tall buildings to accommodate many workers.

Right: In 1929, the Chrysler Building was the tallest structure in New York City.

Legend has it that architect William Lamb held up a humble pencil and decided that that was how his new building should look. When Lamb got the assignment to design the Empire State Building, New York was already full of skyscrapers. How could he make another one that would not only be bigger and taller than all the others, but would also be memorable? What Lamb came up with was a solution that was elegant, simple, and subtle—and turned out to be incredible powerful.

Left: Architect William Lamb wanted the Empire State Building to stand out among the skyscrapers that surrounded it.

Bottom left: According to legend, Lamb found his inspiration for the building in a mere pencil.

Below: Lamb's elegant design proved powerful in its simplicity.

Lamb decided that only the bottom five floors would cover the whole site. The main tower would be set back sixty feet from the street. From the sixth floor the tower soared up seven hundred feet in an unbroken rise to the eightieth floor. Light streamed in from all sides, and no office desk was farther than twenty-eight feet from a big window. It guaranteed a premium rental for office space all the way up.

It was one thing to come up with the design for the world's tallest building. It was quite another to get it built— especially when the financiers behind the Empire State Building told Lamb that they wanted it built in eighteen months, and to be ready for tenants by May 1931.

Top right: Only the bottom five floors of the Empire State Building cover the entire area of the site. Middle: Because of the building's slender shape, workers at every desk would enjoy a view of the city below. Bottom: Lamb, his financiers, and the rest of Manhattan anticipated the building's May 1931 opening.

The challenge for the architect was to build the world's tallest building in record time. When the first steel for the building rolled off the mill in Pittsburgh, there were only thirteen months until the opening day. In six months, 102 floors had to be erected, leaving the winter for finishing off the interior.

There was no room to store all the materials on the crowded site, so they were kept in New Jersey and sent across the river as they were needed. Each piece of steel was numbered, shipped to the site, and hoisted straight in to its correct place. Things were organized so perfectly that it sometimes took as little as three days for steel to go from Pittsburgh to the site and then into the sky as part of the skeleton of the Empire State Building.

Above: Workers rushed to build the colossal building in a record time of thirteen months.

Left: A New Jersey site housed building materials until they were needed for construction.

Top left: Workers were often able to build a floor a day, building the massive structure from the ground up.
Above: The steelworkers, or sky boys, maneuvered steel beams into place with their feet.
Left: Although they performed a dangerous job thousands of feet above the ground, the sky boys were not among the five men who died during construction.

At peak speed, workers put up a floor a day. The stars of the building were the steelworkers, the so-called sky boys. Uncaring about a thousand-foot fall into oblivion, they rode into the air on top of the steel beams, maneuvering them in to place with their feet. Amazingly only five men died during the construction of the building, and none was a sky boy.

As much of the building as possible was standardized and prefabricated, so that when the material arrived at the site it only had to be put together. As the steel frame grew, the outer walls were swung into place and the windows inserted. Limestone and brushed aluminum for the walls were delivered ready-cut and marked, just like the steel. The lower floors were completed even before the steel frame reached the top.

Left: Before the sky boys finished the steel frame's top levels, their coworkers completed the lower floors.

Right: Workers simply had to assemble building materials, which arrived already standardized.

Opposite page: The building's design called for a special mooring mast at the top of the structure. Transatlantic airships could anchor there and unload passengers.

The frame of the building was finished three weeks ahead of schedule, but there was more to build.

A 35-foot mast would be added to the top, so that transatlantic airships could tie up and their passengers disembark. In fact, the mooring mast was one of the looniest building schemes ever planned. Nobody seems to have asked if passengers would want to climb down a gangplank 1,250 feet in the air while the airship swung around in the wind. And anchoring the airship was a nightmare. A rope was dropped in the hope that a man on top of the mast could grab it, but he was in great risk of being pulled up into the air.

Top left: Once anchored, a difficult task in itself, an airship swung in the wind.

Top right: Although the airship anchor idea proved unworkable, the mooring mast itself made the Empire State Building the tallest building in the world.

The whole scheme was quietly dropped. But it was this ridiculous mooring mast that ensured the Empire State Building would remain the world's tallest building for the next forty years.

The building was completed on April 16, 1931. To this day no skyscraper has ever been built so fast. But despite all the publicity it was hard for the owners to fill the building. They ordered lights to be left on at night to suggest the skyscraper was fully rented when it was actually only 40 percent occupied. The building didn't show a profit until well after the Second World War.

Above: The skyscraper opened on April 16, 1931, at the end of the promised eighteen months.
Below: The tradition of lighting up the Empire State Building began when residency was low and owners wanted it to seem full.

Today the Empire State Building stands majestically above the midtown skyline. Only once did New York build anything taller, the Twin Towers of the World Trade Center. Due to their destruction on September 11, 2001, the Empire State Building once again reigns as the tallest building in New York.

Above: The spire of the Empire State Building rises high above midtown Manhattan.

Below: Until their destruction on September 11, 2001, the Twin Towers of the World Trade Center were the only buildings in New York City that rose higher than the Empire State Building.

Above: The building is just one of New York City's many skyscrapers.

THE HOOVER DAM

The mighty Colorado River flows out of the Rockies into the southwest corner of the United States. It's so powerful that it gouged out the Grand Canyon. But in the 1930s the Colorado River was to put America on the map in an entirely different way. This is the story of how the west was won—not by gunmen but by civil engineers.

Right: The Colorado River runs from the Rocky Mountains through the southwest section of the United States.

Left: The powerful rush of the Colorado River flows directly through the Grand Canyon.

In the 1920s demand for water and electricity in the southwestern states was growing fast. Engineers came up with a plan that would solve two problems at once. They would stop the mighty Colorado River in its tracks. Building a dam would create a huge lake that would slake the thirst of the West, and water pouring through the dam would drive turbines to create electricity.

Above left: As more Americans moved to the southwestern states, civil engineers conceived the plan for a dam on the Colorado River. Above right: The proposed dam would harness the river's power to create electricity. Left: The dam would also drive river water into a man-made lake.

But it would have to be the largest dam ever built. Hoover Dam would be twice as big as any dam ever constructed before, and many of the techniques and processes that were used to build it were untried and were therefore experimental.

In 1925 a team of surveyors was sent down the treacherous river to find a location for the dam. After six months they found the spot—Black Canyon, where the river marked the state line between Arizona and Nevada.

The first task was to divert the mighty Colorado River so that the new dam could be built. Workers dug four huge tunnels through the mountains, into which the entire flow of the river would be diverted. The work was difficult and dangerous. But by the time work started America was in the grip of the Great Depression, and millions were unemployed. Men stood in line for the chance to work on the dam for $5 a day.

Above: In 1925, surveyors identified Black Canyon, at the border of Arizona and Nevada, as the ideal site for the dam.

Opposite page: Workers toiled to dig huge tunnels into the mountains to divert the river and make way for the largest dam ever built.

Workmen began stripping the canyon walls of loose rock and material. Spectacular climbing and daring was required to blast away the rock face. Teams of climbers called high scalers did the work.

Next, workers built two temporary mounds called cofferdams, one upstream and one downstream from where the new dam would be. The cofferdams blocked the river and forced it into the new tunnels. Then the water trapped between the two cofferdams was pumped out, and the riverbed was excavated down to the bare rock some eighty to one hundred feet below.

Above: Man-made hills, or cofferdams, forced the river into the newly built tunnels.

Left: After the river was diverted, workers excavated down to one hundred feet below the riverbed's surface.

Above: The dam required more concrete to be poured than any other project before 1933.

Middle: The concrete was poured a little at a time, which caused jagged weak joints.

Bottom: The dam's design of a series of uneven columns keeps the structure strong.

In June 1933 everything was ready for the building of the dam to start. Since the amount of concrete that would be poured was so huge—more than had ever been poured before—the dam could be built only a bit at a time. That meant there would be thousands of joints where new concrete was poured on top of old. Joints are always the weakest part of a construction. To stagger them, the dam was built in a series of irregular columns.

Concrete was poured in blocks. As each block reached its final height of five feet, men sprayed it with water to prevent the concrete from setting too quickly in the desert heat. This was not the only way that engineers hoped to control shrinkage and cracking during the curing of the concrete.

Concrete gives off heat as it sets, as the result of a chemical reaction. In the Hoover Dam the heat would have cracked the dam from top to bottom. To prevent this, pipes were embedded in the concrete, and refrigerated air and water were circulated through them. By time the dam was finished, iced water was running through 586 miles of pipe to cool the dam as the concrete cured. The dam was also riddled with tunnels to assist with the cooling.

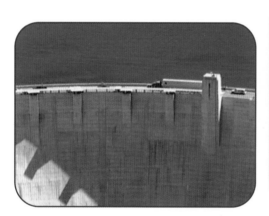 

Above left: Engineers used specific methods to keep the concrete from shrinking and cracking in the intense heat. Above right: Workers embedded pipes, filled with cold air and water, in the concrete to cool it and prevent cracking.

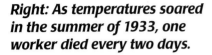
Right: As temperatures soared in the summer of 1933, one worker died every two days.

Left: Heat prostration and dangerous working conditions contributed to the deaths of the 112 workers who died during the dam's construction.

It was more difficult to keep the workers cool. While the dam was being built temperatures were at 115 degrees during the day, falling only to a modest 95 degrees at night. Heat prostration killed one worker every two days during the summer of 1933. In all 112 workers died during the building of the dam.

President Franklin D. Roosevelt dedicated the Hoover Dam in September 1935. Its dimensions are awesome: 70 stories high and a quarter of a mile wide. It took 6.6 million tons of concrete—enough to make a road all the way from the North Pole to the South Pole. The dam was so heavy that it depressed the earth's crust by 7 inches and triggered over 6,000 minor earthquakes. The lake behind it contains sufficient water to supply 5000 gallons to every person on earth. The dam is 45 feet thick at the top, spreading to 660 feet thick at the base. Because the dam is so thick it will take five or six centuries for the core concrete to cure completely.

Above: In 1935, President Franklin D. Roosevelt dedicated the Hoover Dam.

This spread: At a quarter of a mile wide and seventy stories high, the Hoover Dam is a massive structure and a great feat of engineering.

THE INTERSTATE HIGHWAYS

More than the railroad or the airplane, the Interstate Highway System gave America its quality as a nation always on the move. It started in 1956, when the federal government offered to pay 90 percent of the cost of new highways that would provide high-speed travel between cities. The result was a 43,000-mile network of superhighways that became the biggest construction job in American history and created a transportation revolution. The interstates brought cheap travel for goods and people across America. Giant trucks, long distance buses, and a new car-based way of life transformed the country. Drive-ins, motels, and gas stations mushroomed across the continent.

Left: Forty-three thousand miles of highway crisscross the nation in what became the biggest construction job in history

Right: Initiated in 1956, the Interstate Highway System tapped into America's car-based way of life and provided high-speed travel between the nation's major cities.

Building the interstate network took over forty years, but the last piece in the jigsaw puzzle was by far the most difficult. I-70, through the Rocky Mountains from Colorado to California, took fifteen years to complete. It contains the most brilliant stretch of the whole interstate network, through Glenwood Canyon in Colorado. To carry I-70 through the twelve miles of Glenwood Canyon would take three viaducts and thirty-seven bridges. It took amazing engineering skill—and a great deal

of tact—to solve the problems of this environmentally sensitive and difficult canyon.

Above: I-70 winds through Colorado's Glenwood Canyon.

Left: The I-70 project faced many obstacles and took fifteen years to complete

This page: The residents of Glenwood Canyon resisted the building of I-70 because it would interfere with the area's natural beauty.

Glenwood Canyon is on the direct route from Denver to the West Coast. Old Highway 6 ran through the canyon, and it was a deathtrap. A new interstate seemed the obvious answer. But Glenwood Canyon is also a place of great natural beauty and the gateway to the Aspen ski areas. The local residents are well-heeled and vociferous. In the 1970s environmentalists stopped the building of I-70 for twelve years.

In an effort to solve the impasse, a new design team was brought in. The team was headed by Joseph Passoneau, who'd been designing interstates for forty years. This was to be his most difficult challenge. Passoneau spent months walking and climbing the canyon to work out a design. He and his team did detailed drawings to show people how the road would appear. They even put up plywood bridge supports to show where the interstate would run.

Above: Environmentalists halted the building of the Glenwood Canyon stretch of I-70 for twelve years.

Right: Joseph Passonneau led the design team hired to solve the problem of Glenwood Canyon.

JOSEPH PASSONNEAU
Engineering Design

Passoneau's clever solution was to tuck the interstate into the wall of the canyon, and to hide the road behind the trees. The highway soars out from the canyon wall; then, to protect the most beautiful part of the canyon, it crosses the river and dives into a four-thousand foot mountain tunnel. Here, in the Hanging Lake area, there's no highway at all. Even the twenty-four hour control room is buried in the mountain.

The solving of the great Glenwood Canyon problem meant that the interstate network was finally complete. It joined the list of projects built by visionaries who pursued their dreams with dogged determination, creating some of the most breathtaking structures in the world.

Right: Passonneau designed the Interstate with the wall of the canyon along one side and trees along the other. He even hid one of the highway's control rooms in the mountain face.

Left: The interstate rises up into a bridge to protect a part of the canyon. While some super structures are landmarks in themselves, others complement the natural beauty that surrounds them.

GLOSSARY

airship a lighter-than-air flying vehicle, usually a blimp

architect a person who designs buildings

bedrock the solid rock underlying the soil

bends a sometimes fatal condition caused by too rapid a decrease in air pressure after being in a compressed atmosphere

caisson a watertight structure used in underwater or underground construction

cofferdam an enclosure used to temporarily divert water when building a dam or pier

cure to dry out

ecology the study of the relationship between organisms and their environments

engineer professionals who determine how to build something and oversee the process

environmentalist someone who advocates protection of the natural environment

foundry a place where metal is melted and molded into useful shapes

heat prostration a condition of weakness and nausea caused by physical exertion in a hot environment

prefabricate to make in advance

shuttle wheel a wheel used to string the supporting cables on a suspension bridge

skyscraper a very tall building

slake to satisfy or quench

suspension bridge a bridge whose roadway is suspended by cables run between towers

tact a keen sense of what to do or say in order to avoid offending others

turbine a rotary engine that is turned by rushing water

viaduct a series of arches used to carry a road or railroad over a valley or body of water

INDEX

Assembly plant B, 15

Bertholdi, Frederic, 5
Brooklyn Bridge, the, 6–13
    and caissons, 7, 10
    and deaths of workers, 10
    suspension cables of, 7, 11, 13
    towers of, 11

Chrysler Building, 22
Colorado River, 32

Detroit, 14

East River, 6
Empire State Building, 20–31
    mast on, 29–30
    prefabrication of, 27
    steel frame of, 25, 27, 29
    steelworkers (sky boys) on, 26
    time challenge of building, 24, 25, 29, 30

Ford, Bill 16
Ford, Henry, 14–16

Glenwood Canyon, Colorado, 43, 45–46

Hoover Dam, the, 32–41
    cooling pipes and tunnels of, 38
    and demand for water and
        electricity, 33
    dimensions of, 40
    high scalers of, 36

lake created by, 38, 40
and use of concrete, 37–38, 40
workers' deaths, 39

Interstate Highway System, the, 42–46
    and high-speed travel, 42
    influence of, on America, 42
    I–70, the, 43, 45–46
    design and engineering solutions, 43,
        45–46
    and environmental concerns, 43, 45

Lamb, William, 23–25

McDonough, William, 16, 18, 19
Model T, 14, 15

New York City, 5, 6, 11, 20, 22, 23, 31

Passoneau, Joseph, 45

River Rouge Plant, the, 14–19
    assembly line of, 13, 15
    decline of, 16
    and use of living plants, 18
Rouge River, 14
Roebling, John, 7
Roebling, Washington, 10, 11, 13
Roosevelt, Franklin D., 40

Statue of Liberty, 3

World Trade Center, 31